Spoken Ink

The Ink Spot Presents:

Spoken Ink
Written Collection
Volume 1

S. Hope

Spoken Ink

The Ink Spot Presents:
Spoken Ink Written Collection Vol. 1

COPYRIGHT ©2014 S. Hope Jackson

All rights reserved. No part of this book may be used or reproduced in any manner whatsoever without written permission except in the case of brief quotations embodied in critical articles or reviews. For information address BlaqRayn Publishing & Promotions, 134 Andrew Drive, NC 27320

Printed in the United States of America

ISBN-13: 978-0692208298
ISBN-10: 0692208291

Printed by Createspace in 2014
Published by BlaqRayn Publishing in 2014

Spoken Ink

Acknowledgment

A Special Thank You to the talented Poets adding their words to this work of poetic art just as each added their unique and powerful voices to each Ink Spot radio show they attended.

AlidaPoet
Anthony Canela
B.G.B.
Isis Of Poetry
Katherine Felix
Kerry B
Marilyn Renee
Noir Jente
The Empath
Queen Essence
Rare Equivalent
RobbyBabyDarkPoetofAmour
Rosalind Cherry
Shruti Goswami
Topid Qgunsina
Trebor Criswell

Introduction

In commemoration of the 1 year anniversary of the Ink Spot (Spoken Ink) The Ink Spot Spoken Ink Written Collection vol. 1 is an introductory collection of fine writings from 16 talented poets/spoken word artists who were featured on Word "Em Up Radio's The Ink Spot (Spoken Ink) with host Indigo-Soul.

This unique ensemble is a perfect display of crafted ink and a genuine, profound love for poetry.

Spoken Ink

~

Spoken Ink:

Written Collection

Volume 1

~

Spoken Ink

ALI DA POET

Rain On Me:

Rain falls out the sky... fallen upon the heads of those that was once mentally dead.... we was born and breD... we aint scareD, mostly scarreD... too many of our Peoples are locked behind bricks and bars... we all licking old wombs and scars.... we all was born stars...

but they done went too far...

Spoken Ink

LOOTING AND TOOTING DOING DRIVE BYE SHOOTINGS WITH GUNS NO LESS IN THE GHETTOS... YES...

FORGETTING ABOUT AFRIKAN HEROES AND SHE-ROES THAT PAVED THE WAY....

SO FUTURE AFRICAN GENERATIONS COULD LIVE TO SEE A BETTER DAY....

YOUNG LIONS DYING- CRYING- SCOPING- SMOKING FALSE REALITY ....LIVING IN THE EYES OF A DEVIL'S MENTALITY....

BEING KIDNAPPED BYE POLICE FROM URBAN HAVENS...WHERE SYNTHETIC HEAVEN IS BEING SNORTED....BABIES HAVING BABIES THAT ARE BEING ABORTED...

TEENAGE PREGNANCY ON THE RISE AS HEART BROKEN

Spoken Ink

MOTHERS SING SPIRITUAL SONGS, AND AFRICAN LULLABIES...

BUT REGARDLESS TO ALL THE REPRESSIONS THAT'S GOING ON, WE ALL MUST FIGHT BACK AND REMAIN STRONG...

STRONG IN OUR ATTEMPT TO SAVE OUR AFRICAN NATION...

THE ELEMENTAL- SPIRITUAL -CHOSEN ; ONENESS CREATION...

WE ALL MUST FIGHT BACK AND TAKE WHATS RIGHTFULLY OURS, OR ELSE SO MANY HEART BROKEN FAMILIES WILL BE STANDING OVER UNMARKED GRAVES, DROPPING DEATH FLOWERS....

KISS OF DEATH... *Alidapoet*

Spoken Ink

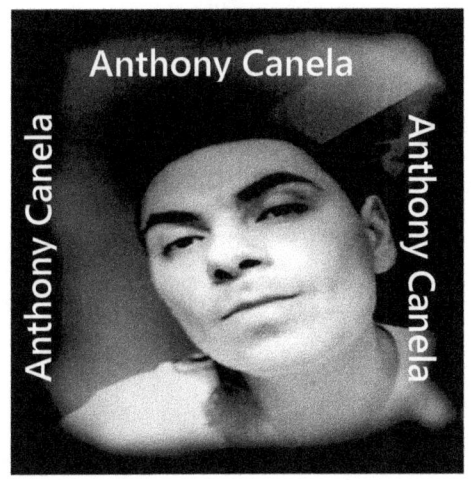

Dr. Ink (er)

I'm a show you the premonition of seeing,

A Hard-to-the-Core demon

That'll barge through the door screaming

When it comes to the Art of Lore

You don't wanna start a War with a carnivore feeding

Spoken Ink

And be receiving a horrible feeling

From this historical reading of revelation

While you're proceeding with hesitation

And needing resuscitation

I'll send 'em back to the Garden of Eden

Starving and breathing

Hard and uneven

From the barbarian beating they'll be receiving

Defeating various nemeses

With this nefarious telekinesis

Scarier than genesis is

The story is just beginning

I'm verbally murdering

Spoken Ink

Nerds that be

Concerned with just cursing & burning me

I'll burst in a free

Verse with a deep

Hyperbole in the 3rd degree

When I vs. an emcee

Unfukin mercifully

I'm not concerned with Gz

Only worried about burning trees

Cuz see, these are young emerging emcees

With firm beliefs in earning cheese

Release flows then

Turn to a freeze posing

Beef provoking

Leaf smoking

Spoken Ink

Reefer choking
Chief Trojan
Who needs (toking/token)
To keep focus...

Bring soldiers
That speak BOLD
& leaving INK SMOLDERING
With needles scrolled in...
A Diseased dosage
Cuz each portion
Of these potions
Will leave emcees
Floating (debris/ the breeze)
Lost in the sea's motion

Only to be found
Drowned down below
Where my flows are forged

Spoken Ink

Underneath the floors of the deepest ocean

Doing my damnedest to be best...

But Secrets SEEK REST in the dreams of SLEEPING CORPSES...

TOXIC FORCES seeping thru Weeping ORIFICES

Reeking with PoISoNoUS osmosis

Is completing this course of metamorphosis

Verbal Pharmacist

Armed with his

Charm and wits

Harming kids with

An arm and fist

Spoken Ink

But I know

The idols they kept

Had turned em into idle skeptics

Burn em with the pyrotechnics

Learning like a bibles lessons

Encrypted with a dialectic

Quickly take another breath kid

Before the words are

Fired in the final exit

Spoken Ink

PENaLIzE
(Pen O'Lies)

Cloaked in a tarred-N-feathered garb

These once shackled ankles still jangle

With the invisible chains that strangle

So I explain the danger in aiming anger at strangers when

Fraudulent Friends

Deceptively disguised as liberals

Rise against criminals

Proliferating pitiful lies and ridicule

Claiming that solving social corruption is a problem

That lies with the individual

Spoken Ink

NOT
this...

Prison INDUSTRIAL complex

But the context has become so complex that,

The systematic deconstruction of urban   stability

Within the city represents symptomatic reflexivity

Where outcasts shunned from society

Reject civility

Swept into projects unwillingly

Forced to project humility

As Worlds of affinity

Swirling in urban activity

Burning so vividly

Spoken Ink

Blurring identity

Burglarize dignity

Haunted by the taunting memories

of what was lost

Daunting is the formidable task

Of breaking out of this cemented caste

Forced into a socially demented class

By pretentious fascists

Herded like cattle in horrendous fashion

Do you have any idea how it feels...

To possess little or no skills

as a direct result of your economically related "social ills"-

Spoken Ink

But be blessed with tremendous passion?

Physically present, but

Mentally absent

Forced to become the

Abscess of a society

That's OBsessed

With assets

And quietly internalize that rage

That's been building in the heart

Beating the Bars of its cartilage Cage

While it silently weeps in the dark?!

Sick with contemplation of so many things it would rather be doing in life

But has no idea where to start

Every siren is an obtrusive reminder

Spoken Ink

Of how this sport of fortune and feud is dire

Infused with losing fighters that refuse to conspire

For the all too elusive fire has been building

With no signs of dwindling

All the while.... the Corporate noose is tighter

Cuz this arrangement or

Modern-day witch hunt-process of enslavement

Predicated through arraignments

Prejudice and payment

By any other name is

Perpetuated by statesmen

Making Oral Statements

Of moral estrangement

Radical conservatism- in my personal opinion

Has become an actual nervous

Spoken Ink

condition

Juxtaposed with xenophobically justifited "supposedly colorblind"

Racially ambiguous- Politically strategic

Totally ambivalent socially anemic...

Bitch-made policies that put a switch-blade to honesty

And RAPED our communities of their GREATNESS and UNITY

Why do you think our country's hegemony started

Building more prisons at precisely the moment that crime rates were falling?

And the amount of institutions built as communities wilt

Within the same timeframe is appalling

Coupled with failing

Spoken Ink

school systems

Designed to fool victims

Into becoming tools of attrition

In a fake war just to make more

New prisons

Someone has to Shoulder blame

We can't blame straight Ghosts

So we play the game of Scapegoats

Shamed into guilt condemned and then hanged

Stripped of our names

Convicted with pain Inflicted

And forget to then blame

The gilded prisons they had built in our brain

Slit open the vein of mainstream society and watch the attritions that spilled down the drain

Spoken Ink

Whether its incarceration, probation, or parole

A friend, a relative, or the brother of someone you know

Is currently under the state's "correctional" control

Armed with ideological weapons that impose

Statutes of limitations on peoples' liberties

Through sections of code

And perpetually scrutinize their direction

To Control the institutionalized methods of conditioning what they know

Penalizing aggression for show

And persecute/(prosecute) their principles to prevent their progression

Till they eventually explode

In the name of, So-called

Spoken Ink

protection

But what are they really protecting, besides their pensions-

And investments?

I'm talking about the

Department of Corrections

Correction, department of deception

Simply a Compartment of Collections

So they fix the news and Twist their views in skewed political elections

Daring you to move in the face of their hypocritical weapons

Interrogating your ethics with loaded questions

Propagating false ideologies' erogenous

Snowballing policies down slippery-slope's

Spoken Ink

Eroticized capitalist fantasies

haven't you had a piece of civil abuse-Liberty's

Subliminal Drug use

& criminology's hypotheses on Gang violence?

What will "We The People"... do

when the only RIGHT that we have LEFT...

Is -"to remain silent"

But even silence is seen as sign of implicit guilt in their eyes

So I fight with their pen of lies

Forever penalized-and stigmatized

Never truly free from their invisible ties

But today I've found freedom inside...

Spoken Ink

For even if they sentenced me

to the penitentiary

for a century,

they still couldn't   censor me!

Anthony Canela

Spoken Ink

B. G. B.

-Midnight Neurosis-

Charcoal wagons show as promised. Holding nightfall in palm

and palm side up

Now calm is none, nowhere.

Fleeing the bleeding suns scorch.

Clumsy and not able

Swallowed whole one half at a time.

Hollow inside a barrage booming Drumming hoof echoes.

Steel stilts trampling chimeras tongue unrecorded.

Spoken Ink

My shadow tangled still.

Upstairs, a stairway uncuffed, spirals

Beyond a boneyard, its belly hanging like beer gut salutes.

Corpus waste!   Rubber spine smells!   Their putrid skull molds!

Choking at once.

My each portion drowned now.

I've weaved this phobia!

Reflections carved knee deep behind weighty eyelids.

Psyche stink!

An author scribing atop a broken brio with bent hanger heads.

An awry appetite grinds my nod into nightmare squash.

Spoken Ink

*And I'm the wrecking ball
leaning toward dusk.*

Poor me!

Hamster wheel victim.

Compulsive vulture disorder.

Borderline agoraphobia.

To slumber:

'Will I ever wave you off?'

Spoken Ink

-Daily-

And she plays
Daily

Undressed in her foreign
Token
She bellows through the haze of
Drunk crazed maunderers

I –
Freely and wondrously
Ponder this exotic
Street soloist
As she romances
Breathing sweet wind
While we lick our wounds
To the usual
Pissy slobber of last night

Spoken Ink

Oblige
My dear

I'm at the whims
Of your pursuit
Daily

Your sweet wind is the morning mist
Bringing this tryst to
Be
Daily

Where the bridge holds its arch humped
Over pigeons talking story
Parcels part by part

Pardon my accent

Spoken Ink

But I'm fascinated
I say

She smiles
Reaching over
Complimenting my features
While
The hostels hunch over
Her natural splash

My Romanian street soloist
She plays
Daily
In a town half mad

And brings me out the sleep
Daily

Breathing wind sweet

Spoken Ink

And foreign

Mainly

For change

I've seen her melody push the rains off

And I've changed my outlook in

A strange place

While the pubs quiet to slow fades

The drunks stumble by

Still she plays

Daily

Waking me

Mainly

For conversation exchange

So it seems

Yet

Spoken Ink

We still meet

Two foreigners

Where her borrowed bridge breathes.

B. G. B.

Spoken Ink

Isis Of Poetry

Scenarios:

(Wake Up and Know the Signs)

It doesn't matter if they lay hands on you or not; don't be fooled There are many types of abuse; here are a few scenarios in case I'm speaking to you...

HE SPEAKS IN MENTAL ANGER: It's 5'o clock and she isn't home I told her like the hands of time; at the drop of my line She'd better answer her phone. I don't put my hands on her physically Mental; that isn't abuse, well at least not to me!

HE SPEAKS IN EMOTIONAL ANGER: Everybody walking around here acting all sensitive You acting all hurt because for your birthday I don't give gifts

Spoken Ink

(as he fires off with his verbal fists) Showing me your poetry; sharing your life stories That's why I had to drop kick you down a notch Nobody cares about you; that stuff is boring You're stupid and if it weren't for me; you'd be and have nothing You should be on your knees thanking God for me Because; I made YOU something Fix your hair and do something to your face; do it "MY" way I don't' want you being seen in public with me looking like a disgrace.

HIS MENTAL AND EMOTIONAL ABUSE TAKES ON ANOTHER LIFE; PHYSICAL ABUSE! SO YOU ARE STILL TALKING, HUH? (AS HE VIOLENTLY GRABS MY FACE IN HIS HANDS) You've said too much, SHUT UP!!! Next comes the blows as they painfully land Viciously grabbing my hair and dragging me into the adjacent room Throws me on the bed;

Spoken Ink

trapping me and sealing my doom Punches begin vibrating throughout my chest, knocking wind from my very last breath What's next?

He says "Look what you made me do, you deserve to be black and blue; you are stupid and at the same time I hate and love you.

Wake-Up and Know the Signs Take note of these few scenarios And leave while you still have time!

Spoken Ink

"The Right Side of Pride"

I am the host

Of a deeply rooted sanctuary

Which now bleeds from

The Right Side of Pride

I am ALIVE!

Than, when punctured;

The color of crimson tide;

Causing me to expire

See,

This shell

used to be bridled

With unintentional lies

Then churned

To manifest

"Richly bitter turned" pride

This would set off

Spoken Ink

An attitude of

"Oh no, thank you I'm fine"

"I'll be okay"

Turning down many blessings of mines

But instead with unpretentious pride

I'd hold my head high

Mentally "Help is for the needy"

I'd wave thanks & good-bye

Narrowly escaping

The humiliation

Of helping me out

Of my destitute situation

Wow...really?

Then I'd turn to look around

Spoken Ink

And when out of plain sight

I'd bow down my head

To hide it from day light

I'd enter a dark space

Where this pride

would anxiously await

And taunt me

regretting

that fateful day

You should have taken that blessing

The little voice would say

So now once again

in pity you lay

Trying to convince myself

My mind riddled in shame

"That blessing will make its way"

Spoken Ink

"Back to me again"...someday

But surely today

my refuge

Possesses proud disposition

The kind that isn't vain

yet holds its position

When you look into my eyes

They smile back to welcome you in

My lips and my grin

Represent that of strength

My shoulders

mountain wide

Now confidently displays

The Right Side of Pride

Ask for help, it's okay!

Today, I can happily

Spoken Ink

Accept Gods giving aid
For it is our purpose to help
and why we were placed

I'm proud of who I am today
My maturity stands to portray

That of a humble conquer
Never too good for my days

For pleasure
would it bring
our ancestors
To know

We're supporting one another
So in vain they did not sew

They slaved

Spoken Ink

on their feet

Planting hope bearing seeds

To allow us Gods blessings

When we are in need

Hands and feet bleeding

And planted on plantations pavement

Tears, blood and sweat

Did they not suffer the loss

Of the

Running

And the gunning

And beating

And starving

And hurting

And belittling

Spoken Ink

And bruising

And criticizing

And cursing

And laughing

At their parents, parents, parents?

I digress, I need rest

SIGH

Our ancestors

Remember

THEY paved the way

We do not have to bear our souls today

But now our children's children are able to say

I stand on The Right Side of Pride

Spoken Ink

Because I'm FREE today!

We all have been enslaved

With pits & caves

Filling up our veins

With mind developing

"I'm too proud to ask for help"

...Ways

Today, I Stand on the Right Side of Pride

Excuse me, may I borrow a cup of sugar

So I can make sweet love for our Tribe?

I. S. I. S.

Goddess of Poetry

Spoken Ink

Katherine Felix

Heart of the Universe

*A small, fluttering soul; questing
in the vast universe*

my spirit soars ever higher...

searching always for the source

Spoken Ink

which in turns flows through all obstacles;

searching for me (and you).

Drawn to its heat

seeking the Gateway;

the path laid down just for me...

my purpose;

my destiny.

Although a lone traveler on this epic journey;

as we each must be;

love unconditional will be my guiding star

the shining reference point

to Home.

Spoken Ink

Those sad souls who lose their way;

meandering   lost in their own reality,

circle aimlessly, but never find

that which we long for most;

for the chord never severed.

Spoken Ink

The Escape

Grey walls of mediocrity

for too long trapped creativity

colours disappeared

while helplessly, watching; one by one;

the muses started dying.

Forcing, praying; just to break though

conformities mask, one tear at a time

gasping for air; an inspirational life-line

choking on old, dull atmospheres

without rhythm or rhyme.

Spoken Ink

The effort – enormous;
to remain true to pure artistry,
clawing through the expected forms of sophistry
not allowing layers of normalcy
to keep us from exploring Truth.

Healing the pains inside
constantly opening fresh wounds
Soul searching fueling creation
As meaning arises from within
symbols & truths; art birthing new beginnings.

The artist within finally emerges
triumphant through re-birthing pains
the surface finally breached –

Spoken Ink

leaking colours

true expression gained in spite of the darkness

this life; art will enlighten.

Katherine Felix

Spoken Ink

Kerry B.

FATHER IN ME

"I'll be right back"

He used to say to me

Or my favorite

"I'll call you back

In a minute"

Patiently waiting

To hear his baritone voice

Music to my ears

Jumping for joy as his young boy

Yet I didn't realize his ploy

Playing me, his parental toy

Counting the hash marks on the walls

On my heart, counting down to the day

Spoken Ink

That his love will free me from

The iron chains of my hatred for him

God teaches to forgive, since he forgave us

For our past, present, and future sins

But how do you recover from stab wounds

From within

Years later, I'm a man now

Screaming victoriously on top of the mountain

I did it! I did it without you, Pops!

No more being ignored if I didn't score

The last touchdown, or how I'd flap more

So I can jump out the gym and you see me soar

Now my tears dried and my

Spoken Ink

body isn't sore.

Yet deep in my core, I didn't realize

Your absence was actually a presence in my soul

Looking into my own child's eyes

I teach, instruct, and inspire

Just the way that I wanted you to

Those times needing you to raise me as a man

Now I'm a king raising a goddess

Her smile is my light, her embrace is my place

Heaven is when she sleeps in my arms

Humbling me as a father

So I thank you, Pops

Thank you for trying to be there

But you see, your absence was really a presence

You became a father in me...

Spoken Ink

MOMENT OF SILENCE

Can we please have this moment of silence?

Heart drops each time I hear police sirens

Black bodies littered in the streets, yet lifeless

Reality TV call it another case of black on black violence

Political tyrants, quick to execute those who are defiant

Yet turn the cold shoulder as Mama and them at the funeral crying

This goes out to my brothers who stay standing in lineups

Keep your head high, even after the indictments

A corrupted justice system, black men continue to be victims

Pissed on like toilet seats, even if

Spoken Ink

they had that right income

Next stop is federal prison, got young men dying slowly as the villain

My heart beats a rhythm to those serving a life sentence

I'm speaking with activism, check the lyricism

Yet I find comedy when so-called Christians spit mad criticism

Yet they've never been in that position, why is it so hard for forgiveness

No wonder the community's broken with all of this division

Another moment of silence

Shout-out to Trayvon Martin and other black boys who died, man

Funny racism gets covered with blindness

Spoken Ink

Especially when my brothers become victims of police violence

My heart goes to Jordan Miles, beaten by cops with his locks ripped out

I wonder with all these killings, do police call it a group discount

Especially with Jonathan Ferrell, who was just asking for help

So they shot him 10 times since he was black and was seen a threat

Protect and serve is the motto, yet they wanna act macho

No wonder when I see the Crown Vics, I ask will I see tomorrow?

Seems their point is hollow, like the lead they spray

Got black men asking when they get pulled over, is this my last day?

Mom always say to always pray,

Spoken Ink

yet I'm always the prey

Looking over my shoulder as I drive in the fast lane

Don't want to feel that ricochet like my other brothers did

So it's for them I wrote these lines and continue to live.

Kerry B.

Spoken Ink

Marilyn Renee

Poetry Warrior

The power of words

can make a person feel good

but if words are misused

they can cut you like

a steel knife

Spoken Ink

go through butter

But fear not
the POETRY WARRIOR
is on duty
fighting for those that
don't let their ink speak for them
putting their pens down
until the ink drys up

well no more
everyone has a style
not right nor is it wrong

don't think your writing
is always the best
so much new and old talents
here to be shared

Spoken Ink

if you never try

you'll never know what

you'll missing

Words give you knowledge

words give a silent voice

a mouth to be heard

loving

caring words

sooth the soul

freaky

kinky

words

bring you some fun

Spoken Ink

caressing

holding

my love

words that

will keep

you home at night

use your words

lightly

PENS UP...

Spoken Ink

WAS LOST BUT NOW I'M FOUND

Have you ever been lost in this world

did you feel as if you were alone

certain things happen for a reason

I been told

Was lost but now I'm found

pain and sorrow tried to hold me down

all my smiles was turning up side down

but now I laugh and go on

no more sad songs

Spoken Ink

time to let my light shine through

be who I'm suppose to be

a strong

Black Queen

Was lost but now I'm found

my eyes used to be blinded

my false kindness

but not anymore

I see the truth

God has made me wiser

I knew he wasn't done with me yet

I'm still a good work in

PROGRESS

Spoken Ink

but I'm WORTH IT

it's good to
Smile...

Marilyn Renee

Spoken Ink

Noir Jente

DROWN

I think that I'll just write...

I

Sitting in my silent room,

talking to my telephone,

about the things I want of you,

about the things I need of you...

...empty, useless epithets

a drowning man hurls toward the shore,

futile struggles curse the tide

that distanced love forever more.

Love's seas now roiled,

Spoken Ink

damning all to the shallows,

who will cry for what is lost?

II

What we felt?

Now blood from a slit wrist

leaking into lukewarm bathwater;

the pinking bubbles

forming rose hearts

from communion with

heavy lid tears.

I want to slide away,

back to the heat

that was us,

stretch these last seconds

back to an eternity,

one that seemed so certain

not so long ago.

Spoken Ink

III

Were I the sinner made saint,

could you love me any more?

Would you be the welcome haven

I have searched through lifetimes for?

Gasping love between these walls,

I think and breathe in fantasies,

while every care we felt before

abates from wounds that slowly bleed...

I am lost in this crimson tide,

helpless as all my love

silently seeps itself away.

I have nothing to write about,

I think that I'll just stop...

Spoken Ink

SWERVED

It is...the deck.

It is...the floor.

It is...the ground,

(or, if you please)

the paved mint,

Spoken Ink

the ass fault.
It's OK to blame it-
you said it was bumpy.
Walk on it because you can,
Ride it to
your bridge to nowhere.
It is part of every destination.
It is responsible
for it all.

It's got potholes
in its soul.
Seasons run
hot and cold,
warm and chill,
for good and ill,
changing for
their own reasons.
It expands, it contracts.

Spoken Ink

It cracks

from inconstant sunshine.

It got abraded in its lanes,

it got grooves and ruts

in its struts,

and trust is now

an iffy proposition

prepositioned by

the weight of cargoes

it was promised

to never bear.

But, swears splinter

and oaths shatter

as fractured routes

no longer matter,

because why worry

about high ways

too difficult to traverse?

Spoken Ink

Go cross-country

before one try

to mend what

whethers weathered,

what stresses stressed.

Run away

to the rough ground,

to the gnarled terrain.

Turn away

from what was smooth

what could be smoothed,

because it's much easier

to swerve.

And now

with both wheels

spinning in mud,

speak of trails

of tears and blood-

Spoken Ink

as if external goads

forced a detour

from the road

willfully abandoned.

Affixed in a ditch

off a lonely freeway

wish very hard

for things

to fix themselves.

Noirjente

Spoken Ink

[Homeless Heart]

Thud, Thud …

Thud, Thud…

The sound of speeding cars,

Over my willful head.

Unaware of my existence.

Un-noticed,

Spoken Ink

Un-dead....

Thud, Thud...

Thud, Thud...

Day in,

Day out.

As I grab another bottle.

To calm my tangible silence.

Frozen, I surface.

To warm my withered hands,

Each vein

Tells a story,

Of a lonely man.

Gathered into one secluded stance.

Distracted by a watery glance.

Spoken Ink

As a tear,

respectively, Slides down my face.

I'm fearful of my unlawful grace.

Disperse my sight...

Alone I fight.

Demonic Fears,

They clench, so tight.

My heart is fading,

Fragile,

As it seems.

Representing a rose,

Clean and pure.

melted into poison,

To drink...

My only cure

Spoken Ink

If I die tonight

Promise me…

Just let me be…

a homeless man,

With my shade of misery.

Spoken Ink

[Winters Morn]

It's a cold winter's morn,

I awoke last night from a terrifying dream.

I dreamed you did not love me anymore.

I Slept awake, drowning in a river of my tears.

My adjacent   limbs are frozen, My breath creates an

Abstract image of the state I emboss.

This coffee is my only form of warmth.

As I think about this vivid sense of departure,

The steam gently floats into nothingness.

Like the cigarette that burns our

Spoken Ink

soul.

Tainted, stained and addictive.

I start to worry.....

Was this just a nightmare. Or did I merely structure truth I alone elude.

I look outside, I try to see your smiling face.

Coaxing me to come out and play in this white, magical snow.

As we melt our hearts with it's gentle embrace of laughter...

To see our kids... Joyful and loved.

Fear can not reach the boundaries of my Heart.

I would die for you.

And yet a part of me does..

Still I cry to have realized,

Spoken Ink

This world can't feel whole without you.

I am like the first snow flake that falls from heaven.

And you, the first to catch me on your silk filled lips.

As I am now one of you,

I have become the glisten in your eyes

Even as the sun fades me away. I vapour as you inhale.

I can feel your rhythmic heart as it skips the love note.

I see, that pain is more stronger than your desire to love.

As the night still falls, On this cold winters night.

Alone I stand outside these icy windows.

The cold expression of it's glacier stare.

Spoken Ink

It's reflection is me, And I alone.

Still I wait.

I cry till I can see you smile again...

The Empath

Music from My Soul

As the melody flows through my soul

I'm transported to a time and space

Where I barely recognize my own face

Flipped, turned and made to swirl

Dealing with the duality of this world

The demons I hide

Me, Hidden behind the melody

The melody that makes me

Spoken Ink

forget

Forget my need for a fix or a hit,

At peace in the music

Music to my soul and...

if only for a second I'm made whole

I gently glide back forth with this bow

Caressing the strings with my fingertips

I give life to this horn with a breath

still stale from my last swallow

This physical realm is so shallow

In the bosom of the melodious sounds,

I am Free

Free from the devils that taunt me

Reminding me of my

Spoken Ink

shortcomings

I am free to express remorse,

for the decisions I made

the beds I've laid

I fly high

If only for a moment

I'm a three piece band on the stage of Julliard

The music and I are one

All pasts deeds are done My soul, my will has won

The light dims and the performance is complete

I'm left with this physical shell we see

Withered and Frayed

In that moment I wish I could stay

Spoken Ink

Engulfed in the vibes of the soulful sounds

This dilemma is so profound

Desperately crying out for change

Pure beauty being expressed through the sound waves

Spoken Ink

The Answer

I always knew I wasn't from this planet. My biggest clue being the fire that raged within exploding into the passion expressed in everything I did.

I am not from this realm for compassion is not an option rather my nature. The transmission I receive tells me to be gentle, kind and to ensure despite all the lies weaved into artistry presented to you .

The name of my home this language doesn't translate, you've labeled it Mars and instead of gaining clarity you'd rather procrastinate. The Fire Planet, we planned it for the purpose of purification yet you transmute the energy sent and

Spoken Ink

refuse to look beyond the stars.

A prisoner in your mind, no longer looking to the divine, neglecting to read the signs, placing all your hope in humankind.

So we were dispatched to your world, I being one, a simple girl to offer understanding to that which you thought you knew. I am not from this planet, I've been placed here as an answer to you.

Queen Essence

Spoken Ink

Rare Equivalent

..Untitled..

cheapened attempts at flattery

coerced into Generic form

you lay.. adjacent to toxicity

licking lies you mutely spawned

shunning the eyes of others

effectively Puncturing what you're made of

a neanderthal of many colours

..you're a Knockoff of your own Trademarked flavor

meshed within the webbing

of your iron-walled catacomb heart

Spoken Ink

you're a Virus that has been self-contained

..begging to smash right through the glass

more than worthy of a cure

you choose to relinquish Love.. of course

as widespread ruin gushes forth

from an unsuspecting suitor

a poison patented to induce infection

to pattern every resemblance to a scorch

you are a nightmare.. unintentionally fashioned

but remember.. I am a vehicle Built for War

never unheard are your sighs

LXXXIII

Spoken Ink

nor every desperate grasp at joy
your Mirror's Reflection is

imploring you..
..to See between these lucid lines

the air in your lungs is thinning
diminishing in hushed whispers
so you latched the lid upon
your self-filled music box
failing to notice.. the dancer
Inside.. is Still spinning

Spoken Ink

..Wings..

I like the look of his shoes beside mine

they coincide.. the way his walk seems to match my steps in time with my own stride

I like his pulse banging heavy

beating steady.. with a dialect that only mine can hear by vibe of a privately specialized frequency

I like his hands holding mine

intertwined.. fitting perfectly & clutching tight with a grip that never weakens along with the look that's in his eyes

This boy has Wings.. Yes we are Synchronized

eyes on the same prize & shootin higher than dope.. we fly

we rise.. illuminating mixed

Spoken Ink

medleys at the ready to the sound of explicitly accentuated rhymes

borderline electrified.. he touches more than just my thighs

he devours my inner spirit while he eats upon & satisfies my Mind

which I reciprocate.. I reflect his shine

with immense love & dedication & the intentional intensity of blistering Fire

---

when distance doesn't mean a thing

because he knows it's Him I'm sitting right Beside

he gives me strength in the face of other people's adversity

when the air becomes too thick

Spoken Ink

to breathe.. he gives me breath
& his return is All of Me

I like the way the light hits his speech

every time he speaks.. my heartbeat peaks til my blood heats & by way of a sweet peach ripened I fall at his feet

I like the smile within his voice

the way it's not by choice.. seeping through my circuitry until it broils & becomes adjoined

I like his lyrics flowing deep

always within reach.. razor edged every time & throat slicing with the Frees

I like his self assured sentences

an accelerant to Excellence.. sealed & cemented with his own

Spoken Ink

familiar personalized expressions

This boy has Wings.. spanning Multiple dimensions

potential never lessening within a mind forever focused upon excelling.. it's endless

Epic.. & Still swelling.. creativity is the foundation that bleeds beneath a Superior mindset

what he represents? Lyrical Death.. always willing to obligingly contest upon the denial that he's been blessed

Realness at it's best.. making other contenders attempts appear Mute.. he's Foolproof

which is why he rightfully possesses the title of being deemed Shatterproof

---

when distance doesn't mean a thing

Spoken Ink

because he knows it's Him I'm sitting right Beside

he gives me strength in the face of other people's adversity

when the air becomes too thick to breathe.. he gives me breath

& his return is All of Me

I like his style & dress sense

his entire personality at Length.. perfectly addressed.. always fresh with just the correct amount of Intense

I like the manner in which his actions reside

knowledge hiding behind bright eyes luminescent like shining diamonds.. all the while with such passion burning alongside

I like him in Black & White

it's just right.. matching his

Spoken Ink

attitude & complimenting the way I see him.. in Highlight

I like his firm physique

arms that could carry me.. wrap my waist & lift me up to sweep me off my feet with Certainty

This boy has Wings.. he is my Angel most Certainly

preserved are my affections because I see them to be reserved deservingly.. personally

in this eternity.. he has ignited the Fire within me both internally & externally

merely verbally.. maybe one day his eyes will return the same reflection that my Own see

he is unique in every way.. although a shame he doesn't See me.. or perhaps thinks that I'm Beneath him

yet Still.. he remains close in my Dreams

Spoken Ink

---

when distance doesn't mean a thing

because he knows it's Him I'm sitting right Beside

he gives me strength in the face of other people's adversity

when the air becomes too thick to breathe.. he gives me breath

& his return is All of Me

..This boy has Wings..

Spoken Ink

Robby Baby
Dark Poet of Amour

At A Distance

At a distance I feel it,

the pull of the unnameable,

and I've come to realize that in this life,

it is the ineffable that draws us most,

Spoken Ink

we fall most under the power of
unnameable things.

For love is what most moves us,

passion is what drives us,

the joys of art are what compel
us to create,

as we name God or the Universe
in   previously unmade and
unnamed things.

I feel the pull of it,

the heft and weight of its gravity,

as those immaterial and
sometimes unnameable things,

their gravity presses upon me to
take action,

as love pulls at my heart strings,

and I feel invigoration of passion
as fire in my bodies veins.

Spoken Ink

I do not want to sully them in the naming of them,

do not want to try to give them platonic form,

rather,

I will let them rest in the cave of allegory,

existing as the shadow shapes that we first see,

that we first gaze upon when we perceive of these things.

I will not name them in forms of technicality,

I will not take their magic away with abstruse and long winded names,

rather,

I shall let the names the universe already gave them be gleaned through verses of poetry,

musicality of notes,

Spoken Ink

and brush of painters stroke of color,

and I will let myself drift in the meaning of them,

these powerful entities that are immaterial and sometimes unnameable things...

Spoken Ink

I Dream of Satellites

I dream of satellites,

as their mysterious orbits intersect with my thoughts,

ellipses of cosmic engrams transiting in me,

speaking to both the Venus and Mars of my soul.

I dream of these satellites in daydreams at day,

and I look upon them at night,

as I wonder upon them,

wishing I could wander as they do,

as they careen through the inky void of space.

What a dream is the dream of satellites,

Spoken Ink

as they make the music of the spheres in minor keys,

as their orbits intersect with each other,

tugging at my soul as the moon does tug at the sea each night.

I want this dream to be mine forever more,

as scores and scores of dreams,

they pockmark my mind,

oceans of thought in my soul as numerous as the marina found upon them,

those wanderers of the night that cross into the parallax of my vision,

leaving both my mind and soul so utterly refined.

I hope to impart this dream to everyone,

Spoken Ink

this dream of mysterious bodies
that hold the history,

the record of existence upon
their bare and rocky skins,

and as I look upon them now,

I ask you,

oh fellow wanderer,

what is it that satellites dream?

Robby Baby Dark

Poet of Amour

Spoken Ink

Rosalind Cherry aka Cherry Bomb

There Lies Soul~!

There Lies Soul~!
there she was in
position there were powers
that even she felt

Spoken Ink

that was taking
a hold to her
soul.

It was when she
went upon the forest of
darkness to face her
fears it was then
she would know her
Womanhood.

She was single out for tribe.

She seen the
darkness of the path of
of one side
telling her to seek
and you shall find
that moment

Spoken Ink

to see the golden
side.

How can this be?
for she was the
this stranger to the
unknown she walked the
path along it
was days at a time
she was thirsty
in no thoughts of
food.

Still she could not stop.

She was beaten and
worn out through out
her travels, blisters upon
her body and feet, as the

Spoken Ink

branches whipped and tore
upon her body
torture.

She prayed along the way.

Almost blinded by
the Sun" not paying
attention to her
flesh of her skin
for she was going through
the darkness that
made her see she
make it through the
storm.

She hard this
roar sound that heading
towards her then

Spoken Ink

her body begin to
crumble she fell
to the ground
now she turning
golden brown image
to the other
side.

Two shade of
this to stand the
test not to
be the best let
the forest of
unknown known she
could survive she rise
Queen stood beauty
before herself the image
of two side
beast.

Spoken Ink

Nature was her witness
she composed herself
never to
question her appearance
she stood before
her throne of
wood seat fitted for
the Queen of the
forest.

The Lies Soul~!

She delivered untamed
soul that once lost
she believed in herself
again, to know
in her position she now
found her inner peace

Spoken Ink

of her foundation

of her soul

stand her ground

here she comes the

Queen…

Spoken Ink

Even In Morning~!

Even in morning~!
her soul was dim she
was fight her own
fate as the rays
were appearing she
felt nothing she
sat in thoughts of
nothing"

Circumstances left her
numb she was
fighting forces of
many things if
she had no
answers for any
more?

Spoken Ink

Feeling as if
she was in this
world turning
from one place being
shut down right after
another felt as
if she was used up
tired of everything
enough"

Her life was falling apart.

The winds were
blowing shifting back
and for through
her soft skin
she bowed down
her burdens begin to
much to bare

Spoken Ink

praying"

She thought if
she had this
last chance to get
it right what
would become of
her?

She begin to
think about when was
the last time
she felt her
own soul when
was last time
she smile or even
laugh"

Emotions were going

Spoken Ink

wild roaming every
where what was of
importance she begin to
hate so she caught
herself sitting there
thoughts to be drifted
away if only
she really tried
harder"

She praying take
away the pain
tearing her up she
decided this was
to be the place
for all of this to
be removed by the
Ocean"
Kept to many

Spoken Ink

things lock up
inside far too
long in search for
miracle"

In hopes as
she rise the
Sun shall set she
shall rise to claim
back what was
missing"

For this beautiful
Woman who needs
to reclaim back
her life for only
she and God
share this
together"

Spoken Ink

Pray and share
lift your head start
your life over
now before you
become that lost
soul left
out towards the
Ocean"

Rosalind Cherry

Spoken Ink

Shruti Goswami

Crossroad

At the cross road of life,

I wait an eternal wait,

Love eluded me, deserted me long ago.

I waited for wisdom to dawn,

Spoken Ink

But the mind believed otherwise.

I tried hard, and my heart yielded,

The mind refused to budge.

Confused, like one lost amid dense woods,

Of artificial walls and barriers;

I knew I had the strength,

When everyone else left me to die.

Friendless, forsaken, lonely and broke,

But everyday to the call of birds,

My mind still awoke.

Introspection was all that I had,

To find what kept me alive.

Faith it was, in humanity,

That makes me thrive,

I am at a crossroad,

Spoken Ink

I am not ready to die,

Wings of faith and warmth of hope,

I know that I will fly.

Spoken Ink

The Golden Orb

It's another sunset, a beautiful one,

But the burning orb, throbs in pain.

Innumerable beauties that once made her rich;

Wine red sunrises and golden sunsets

All in vain.

The devastation, the havoc, that the body bears,

Intolerable now, a deep unrest,

And so amid dark clouds looming in the sky,

Volcanoes erupt intermittently, once at rest,

Threatening to obliterate every single form of life.

The golden orb is melting away,

Spoken Ink

And with it will come an end to our stay,

Let humankind rise up to the occasion,

Let the sun glow and the earth thrive,

Amid new hopes, and a new longing

For yet   another bold and beautiful day.

Shruti Goswami

Spoken Ink

Topid Qgunsina

OUT OF BATTLE

She looks deep in herself
All she see's is pain
No friends, no families
To take away her pain
Bullies are terrorist to her

Negative thought was only friend
She always welcome every single second's
Because no privilege for positive thought
Her situation was favourite topic of society
She decided to become a

Spoken Ink

drunker

Maybe society will close her chapter

But no,society will always be society

She stopped drinking

And knew courage was her only option

She embrace it and became unbreakable

And she hold-on to her dream

The night she made it

She won the battle

And out of the battle

Because the battle is no more in her existence

Spoken Ink

BEAUTY

Words are powerful than weapons

Use words as tools not weapons

Use it to heal

Not to create metal illness

Those voiceless street children

Use words to give voice back to them

Because word is voice

Plant the word love in society

So that,society can be an ocean of love

Not ocean of hatred

Save the unborn generation today

With love and change

Because you are today

That will give birth to tomorrow

Spoken Ink

So tomorrow must not be fill with sorrow

Must not be ugly but must be a rose

Because there's peace in beauty.

Topid Da Poet

Spoken Ink

Trebor Criswell

The days we never had...

Your eyes are like Acadia

Up north traversing the Maine shore

Where we used to spend summers that seemed like

days of millennium

a few miles outside of Bangor

On mossy sleeved summit of granite and sandstone we stood

Thieving gulls at thunder canyon

and that ever present crackle of evergreen wood

I wish that I could take you

To sunset rock

And the candlestick bowling lanes

Spoken Ink

To the white sand beaches

Where stucco cliffs loom in shards

guarding over each his own

In waters that scream pins and needles

Bare feet in the white foam

And that horizon on the ocean

That stretched like limbs of the sky

miles

after napping overtime

I wish you could see the view beyond the trees from the cabin porch swing

And spend nights remembering

How the shadow of fire skipped off your ripe skin like butterflies in the belly of tonight's ending

As we snuggle for warmth under blankets of memories

Spoken Ink

When we were just kids

And certain things bared no importance

Beyond innocence

Or engines that traveled over those gravel roads

To immortalize the beginning of these sentences

Upon ink stain and pen laden page

I'll remember

And cherish those days we never had...

Spoken Ink

Lacquered Lips:

I wanted to drink you away,

but the bottom of the bottle didn't take you

Wanted to ferment in this pain

So your face kept me up at nights wasted

Cordials didn't cure

The lacquer of liquors lip-smack

just lapped and sipped and spatted and spit

until the first spill of last pour

Sent me stumbling on the shudder of muscles spasms gripping

Four

more

steps

to the bathroom

Spoken Ink

in an unfortunate turn of what felt like a century in my head spinning

lunging

urgently

forward

How many days are spent bent over on knees of last nights prayers

waves breaking crest of oceans as we try to flush away the landing

Understanding the   past

Has outlasted it's stay

I'm betting on anything that will satisfy that craving

A plan for the future?

Never set in place

For a soul travels all the universe

By body

by spirit

Spoken Ink

and page by written page

Turned by licked finger

and a lingering desire to write on until day break

For I keep my namesake on sleeves that hearts once held as home

The pen another ventricle bleeding to cycle necessary components

Dripping Ink spots

thick as blood drops from veins too skinny and frayed

Tipped from top of ball pointed at filled page

These days away from you have solidified what I've been saying

all these years

You were the tears I wish I had never cried

The lips I let lap and sip at the sap of my saddlebags and inner

Spoken Ink

thighs

The decade I spent pretending lit embers would some day die

The pain I wish I had never let antagonize my pride

So now the burn hits my heart

The sour mix and whiskey starter

The farther I drifted the closer you tried to keep me threaded

Now your memory splashes the bottom of way too many glasses emptied

and left for dead

Spoken Ink

The Ink Spot Presents:

Wishes you will enjoy reading these words and verses from the pens and souls of these very talented artists, as we also hope a love for poetry grows ever deeper in your minds and hearts. If you are not a lover, we think these poems may change your entire perspective...

ENJOY

Indigo-Soul

www.ingramcontent.com/pod-product-compliance
Lightning Source LLC
Chambersburg PA
CBHW071515040426
42444CB00008B/1662